Communities

Libraries and Information

C000037639

Items should be returned on or b
shown below.

An item

Karlik
Encounters with Elemental Beings

Karlik

Encounters with Elemental Beings

Ursula Burkhard

Translated by David Heaf

First published in German in 1986 as
Karlik: Begegnungen mit einem Elementarwesen
by Werkgemeinschaft Kunst und Heilpädagogik,
Weissenseifen, Germany
First published in English by Floris Books in 2017

 Also available as an eBook

British Library CIP Data available
ISBN 978-178250-444-3
Printed in Great Britain by Bell & Bain, Ltd

Contents

Introduction

In his book *Theosophy,* Rudolf Steiner speaks about the variety of beings which are in people's surroundings but which cannot be perceived with the senses. He says:

Those who are capable of spiritual perception do perceive these beings and can describe them. The lower beings of this sort include all those described by seers as salamanders, sylphs, undines and gnomes. It should be unnecessary to mention at this point that such descriptions cannot be taken as literal depictions of the underlying reality. If they were, the world they refer to would not be a spiritual world but a crudely physical one. In fact, they illustrate a spiritual reality that can only be described by using metaphors and images. Individuals who accept sensory perception alone as valid will believe these beings to be the product of superstition and of an imagination run wild. This is totally understandable. These beings will never become visible to physical eyes because they have no physical bodies. The superstition, however, lies not in believing these beings are real but in believing that they appear sense-perceptibly. Beings of this sort help to build up the world, and we encounter them as soon as we enter higher territories that are inaccessible to our physical senses. The truly superstitious people are not those who take these descriptions as images of spiritual realities, but both those who believe in their actual physical existence and those who deny the spirit because they feel obliged to reject the sensory images.[*]

St Paul writes in his Epistle to the Romans (8:19):

For creation waits in eager expectation for
the children of God to be revealed.

In nature, only beings can wait in eager expectation. So does he mean it is beings such as gnomes, undines, sylphs and salamanders that are waiting in creation?

---

[*] *Theosophy,* Chapter 3, V. The Physical World and its Connection to the World of Souls and Spirits, pp. 157f.

Image and Being

He is there in front of me on the table, a small wax figure. When visitors see him they say, 'That is a gnome.'

Actually, I ought to be glad that they recognise what I was trying to make. My encounter with a real gnome had prompted me to try it. But there is still something rather unsatisfactory which is hard to put into words. Their statement 'That is a gnome', fixes the elemental being here in our world and makes my wax figure into something of a finality. That is also why questions immediately arise when reflecting on it, such as, in reality is he large or small? When you become aware of him, is it like the delicate tickling of a fly?

In reality he is neither big nor small; he is not at all measurable. In fact he is neither visible to the eyes, nor tangible to the hands. That is also why it is impossible for him to tickle me delicately like a fly, although he does like to tease people. My skin can neither feel nor be tickled by something which does not exist materially. In reality he cannot stand on the table so rigidly; he takes up no space at all and is not bound to any place. Therefore I cannot at all show what he really is like.

So in spite of this, why have I even tried to make a portrayal of him? Visitors ask me this question when they observe my wax figures, and I often ask myself the same question.

The figure on the table in front of me points like an image or a gesture to the being 'gnome'. It is an expression of my experience, of my own encounter with him. But for other people, it cannot substitute for their own perception. Whoever perceives a living being or an object with outer senses, and then forms the right thoughts about them, arrives at clear concepts. However, those who try to do the same with portrayals of elemental beings create false ideas of a world as if composed of rarefied matter comparable with the outer world. A world envisaged in such a way is ghostly, not spiritual.

The figure, which like a picture or a gesture, points to the being 'gnome' and thus is the expression of my encounter with him, conveys to the unprejudiced observer a mood, a new feeling. I could have spoken about a gnome instead of modelling him. But then it would not be possible to give a naturalistic description. I would have to speak in similes. Our language is better suited to describing the outer, visible world. Anyway, soul experiences belonging to an inner invisible world can usually only be spoken about pictorially. But such pictures are sometimes so habitual that we hardly any longer notice them as such.

Someone who is having a hard time has 'a load on their mind'. We cannot weigh the burden which oppresses them and the relief after the burden is lifted is not measurable. What cannot be said in metaphors or similes can be conveyed by glances and gestures or perhaps by the tone of voice, hesitation, a longer pause or an eloquent silence. And then it may happen that the person who is listening takes hold of the hand of the silent one and understands what cannot be put into words through everything that points to it like a picture. The listener does not understand it with the intellect but by empathising with the other person.

We can picture something akin to this in the encounter with an elemental being, an empathising experience with the mysterious workings of nature. This empathy can become so strong that it intensifies into a sort of picture and indicates something of the nature of a being. Whoever tries again and again to experience these first fleeting impressions, thereby attuning himself with nature, gradually progresses from the picture, from what is *like* a being, to the being itself. Only deep love and devotion can lead to this goal.

11

A seven-year-old boy had an inkling of what I am trying to describe. I gave him a wax model of a little gnome from the bog near Todtmoos. He frequently talked to the gnome and once said to his mother, 'You know, this is only a model. The real gnome is inside, so we cannot see him.' Through the image, he let himself tune in with what was invisibly living within or beyond it.

Adults find it hard to distinguish the image from the being so naturally. They do not feel like attuning themselves. They would rather have instant information and arrange such information obtained superficially in their pre-existing world outlook. We should practise empathising perception daily. It will become a power in us that is like something alive and growing, something akin to the invisible workings of nature, and therefore can lead to an encounter with the hidden world of beings.

Possible Ways of Meeting

There are several possible ways of encountering elemental beings. I want to arrange them in three parts, following Rudolf Steiner's path of training, but at the same time I want to describe them as they were accessible to my own subjective faculty of perception. Of course, whoever, like me, is still at the beginning of this path can only speak about the first steps and thus encourage others to have their own experiences.

1. Imagination

The image of a being within me is a soul experience. I myself am still deeply involved with it. The more I learn to empathise selflessly with the being, the more the image loses its subjective character. More and more distinctly does it then mirror the being. The initial human outlines of the image disappear. I must learn to hold back my own personal wishes and ideas so that it can reveal itself properly within me. Memories of children's books or mythological forms easily mingle with personal experience. In order to give form to these beings, work on myself – cleaning the mirror – is more important than the perfection of the mere technique of modelling with wax.

The pictorial experience of an elemental being is like a dream that awakens to a new consciousness within me. This does not just happen to me like an ordinary dream, because I can learn to master it and control it like my sense perceptions.

2. Inspiration

I can also meet elemental beings through conversations. When they speak, I don't hear them directly, because they do not have voices like human beings or animals. It is more as if someone has just said something and does not continue speaking. What I have heard lingers in me, lives on in me, and is already on its way to becoming my own thoughts so that I can translate it into human words. Perhaps it is like this because these beings do not speak a human language and are not limited by space and time. We speak into the space between one another and uttering a sentence takes place in time. Gnomes speak within me, conveying their thoughts and feelings without forming sentences.

They do not speak to me from a position outside me, but convey their message into me in such a way that it is like a thought within me, one which I do not develop myself, but which I have received as a gift. Our language has expressions like 'sudden idea' or 'brainwave' for such thoughts. Probably likewise storytellers of old experienced the wise words which gnomes handed down to us in fairy tales and legends.

The fact that for human experience the speech of the elemental beings appears to comprise words and sentences, is related to the pictorial experience which leads to the portrayal of such beings in the form of figures.

3. Intuition

I also know of joyful experiences, free from all hint of word or picture. But they are rare and I feel as if they are great gifts.

I can experience myself within a being and the being within me; we simultaneously interpenetrate one another. We are two beings, and yet in this state like one. What is not physical in me unites itself with a being which can in no way be perceived by the external senses. And through this very unity I can recognise what the being is like in reality.

15

Such experiences are hardly comparable with our everyday experiences. For me, the most accurate analogy is music. The tones of the various instruments of an orchestra unite in harmony. We do not hear them separately, they interpenetrate for our perception. They are in harmony, but nevertheless remain as individual notes. After they have played together, we can allow each individual instrument to sound and thus hear each note of the former harmony as an isolated note, as something existing for itself alone. By analogy, perhaps this experience gives rise to the idea that elemental beings interpenetrate and form a unity, but nevertheless remain individual beings. And similarly, human beings too can unite with a spiritual being, so that later, once again separated from it, the being is then experienced pictorially in the mind or speaking within.

I have tried so far to make myself and others conscious of how it is possible to perceive beings which are not accessible to our senses. Whoever wishes to become conscious of something can only do so through clear thinking. But whoever wants to befriend elemental beings, must approach them with love, participate in their joys and sorrows, just live with them as one does with rocks, plants, animals and one's fellow human beings. Of course, it would be unthinkable to befriend a person whilst one is continually analysing the nature and possibilities of the encounter with them. But with invisible friends, it is nevertheless necessary to devote oneself to thoughts that increasingly thoroughly test how we perceive them. Only thus can we clean the mirror in our soul, so that they may show themselves clearly and we are not taken in by some kind of delusion.

I should like to tell all those who have been carefully considering what I have said so far and been clearly thinking over it, about personal meetings and experiences with elemental beings. Elemental beings yearn for encounters with people and therefore I will try through my descriptions to point the way into their world.

Fleeting Encounters

As a child, I liked to play with dwarves and elves. I knew and understood them. As I was born blind, grown-ups and teachers had to reconstruct for me the physical surroundings by systematic visual instruction. For the 'other world', as I called it, I did not need anyone to explain it to me. Sometimes I wanted to tell adults about it, to share my experiences with them. While I was still young, they listened patiently to me and kindly gave me all their time and attention. But when I was older they considered it necessary to try to talk me out of this 'other world'. They explained that I must learn to distinguish what is truth from what one only pictures in one's imagination. To support their assertion that this other world of mine was not true they said, 'There is nothing about elves and dwarves in the Bible. And believing in what is not in the Bible is sinful.'

But I did not just *believe* in these beings, I *experienced* them, and thus I began to suffer my first big problem in life. What I was unable to see, I had to believe from the adults, and they knew exactly what was and what was not truth. But what I myself perceived was not in the Bible and therefore was a sin – it was not permitted to believe it or even to experience it; that was a really difficult problem for a child.

My friends from the 'other world' were still there, but when we played together, I did so with a guilty conscience and often forced myself to turn away and forget or suppress them. So there were only fleeting encounters, and I did not reach any real friendships with elemental beings. As a result, without realising it, I learned two important things in this period: I got used to keeping quiet about inner experiences, which were all too often talked to death; and by turning my back on elemental beings, I trained myself to ignore them and concentrate on other things. This was important: without this exercise of will imposed on me, I would have become a toy and not a master of my inner experience.

The Breakthrough

The breakthrough began when we were reading Goethe's *Faust* in the final year at school. The images and characters of the drama gripped me so strongly that I was no longer able to suppress my own inner experience. Shortly afterwards, when I was a student, I gave up any religious scruples and the guilty conscience that went with them. During lectures on early English literature, I learned about the Christianity of the Irish monks and its close connection with nature. I was able to relate to that. I felt released by these early Christian figures and the spirit of their time.

From then on, I enjoyed family outings without restraint. While the others were taking in the beauty of the landscape with their eyes, I discovered through my inner perception beauties they never dreamt of.

Once we were sitting in a meadow on the edge of a wood. It was in Alsace. A gnome walked slowly out from among the trees. He approached me and looked at me with astonished eyes that grew wider and wider. I looked at him with my inner eyes.

'Can you see me?' he asked.

'Yes,' I replied.

Whereupon he shook his head, stood for a while speechless, then went thoughtfully back into the wood. I realised: gnomes too have lost their contact with us human beings. So it is reciprocal; we must get used to each other again.

At that time it was not clear to me why we can experience an elemental being in this way, as if it is moving in space. Now however, I expect it is something like this: a gnome is experienced pictorially in a particular place because he concentrates on it. Through my inner experience of nature, the woodland gnome felt drawn to me. I saw this pictorially, as if he were approaching me. He needed to get clear in his mind what was happening between us. I experienced his paying attention to me as my being looked at. That is how pictorial experiences can be explained and, our clear thinking will dispel any notion or superstition about a material but rarefied spiritual world.

The more confident I felt in my contact with elemental beings, the more I accepted the encounters simply as they happened. Spontaneous experiences enabled more intimate relationships with my invisible friends.

I owe my acquaintance with a water-splasher to having been on a family picnic in the Bernese Oberland. I was sitting by a little stream listening to the murmuring and splashing. There amid the rushing, something was making a sound that was reminiscent of church music. It resounded from a strange, misshapen stream-goblin. I became deeply reverent and listened in awe. I was wondering if such beings also prayed, whereupon a laugh gurgled from his belly and his music changed to a sort of waltz. He was teasing me and playing with my moods. The music of nature in the rushing of the water, which I heard only inwardly, originated from him.

The water-splasher became one of the children's favourite characters in my fairy tale, *Schnips.**

I learnt more and more of the riches and of the variety in the realm of elemental beings. I made friends and acquaintances amongst them. Many I got to know only fleetingly. I have never succeeded in having a lasting relationship with an elf or a water-nymph. Gnomes however, seem to long for friendships with people more strongly.

I would have liked others to take part in my experiences. But I could not speak about them in such a way that they were able to understand. Fairy tales seemed to me to be the most suitable medium.

* *Schnips: Ein Zwerglein macht Dummheiten* (a gnome gets up to tricks).

23

But adults no longer take fairy tales seriously. They must be interpreted. In doing so, one forces the vivid living imagery through which elemental beings show themselves in fairy tales into a dead intellectual construct. The fairy tale images fade and are only symbols or allegories. It is not easy to reunite the separate worlds of elemental beings and people.

The First Helper

The enchanting world of elemental beings was increasingly revealed to me. This experience was wonderful and full of marvels. But it was also dangerous. I began to feel lonely among people who were not interested in my experiences, and because of this I involved myself more deeply with my friends in the invisible world.

At that time I was able to fly. This is what I called my ability to leave my body in full consciousness and, freed from it, 'enjoy' the spiritual. These excursions probably had a certain similarity to trips which many young people now take with the help of drugs. Jacques Lusseyran made the apt comment in his book *And there was Light* – blindness can work like a drug. The tendency to live wholly introverted is intensified by loss of visual stimuli and one has difficulty in maintaining a balance between the outer and the inner.

While 'flying' I especially liked to visit fairies and elves, appreciating how they hover, continually changing, always moving and weaving beautiful flowerlike patterns out of light. Their surging, resounding radiance and their ever-changing, glittering spectacle can confuse and delight. At first I just abandoned myself in the wonder and enjoyment of it, instead of getting to know the role of these beings. In everything they do there is wisdom and purpose.

The flying, a state of detachment, would certainly have made me ill, had I not been sent a helper straight from the realm of the elemental beings. A root-man.

He was still somewhat attached to a root which I had found near Chartres. The root had a curious gnome-like shape. By feeling the root with my hands, I was able to connect myself with its hardness and gnarled forms. And out of the firm and gnarly root the root-man spoke more and more clearly to me, just as an elemental being can sometimes speak to a person from one of my wax figures (earlier I mentioned the seven-year-old who experienced the gnome of Todtmoos in this way).

The root-man was tough and gnarled; he looked rather like his root. What he said was not pleasant, not like floating in the world of the fairies: he sounded rough, brusque and sullen. But that was exactly what I needed. I needed pulling up. 'Stop flitting about! You're not a fairy. Take root! We've all got jobs to do. We do something for the earth. Remember that!' What he said to me was something like that. You cannot imagine how cross these gnarly fellows can get.

My encounter with the root-man brought about an awakening. I realised that he was right and that now I had to do what I had learnt as a child, namely look away from these wonderful beings of light. However, this time it was not from fear of the do's and don'ts of the adult world, but out of my free will. I *wanted* to attend to my duties here on earth. I set out on the path with plenty of courage and confidence. I did not know then how hard that path really is.

As the root-man had ordered, I cast off my wings. That is to say, I engaged with everyday life in such a way that I lost the possibility of going on more 'trips'. I began to study my surroundings with my remaining senses, and then only at certain times did I apply myself, equally deliberately and earnestly, to my inner experiences.

I owe much to my encounter with the root-man. For his part, he became more and more free of his root. I do not know whether this was just how I experienced it or whether he in fact did this, because the root became dry and withered. Now I could talk to him without having the root near me. Later, a child asked me for the 'funny gnome root'.

'Give it to him,' he commanded, and I obeyed.

Shortly afterwards he said goodbye to me. He had told me what he had to impart and I had understood.

His job was done. I could not ask him where he was going. He seldom answered me when I wanted to know something. Despite that, I asked him to tell me whether there was something I could do for him.

'Let me live within you and don't forget that you need roots,' he replied.

Thus I endeavoured to stand more and more firmly on the earth. This 'taking root', as he is called it, was difficult for me and has become one of my life's tasks. From my conversations with the root-man I learnt that everything which comes to meet us is a task. With each revelation we have from the spirit world comes an increase in our share of responsibility for what happens here on earth. Instead of the former wings, now it was a matter of bearing this burden, feeling its weight and, in contrast to that, sensing my own powerlessness. In such insights, the root-man continued to live in me, just as he had requested – tough, hard, awakening. He also lives in my wax figures and fairy tales, which are expressions of the seriousness of such encounters. All my efforts at portrayal, by telling stories and modelling, aim to emphasise the common task of humanity and elemental beings in their service on the earth.

A Faithful Friend

The seriousness of this encounter and my inability to convince people of our task in common with the elemental beings led me to doubt myself. I felt clumsy, a nobody. 'Not a real person', as I used to tell myself. I was no longer equal to these inner questions and the daily work which was made more difficult by my handicap. As often happens in such situations, I became ill. As a result of that I had the time and the peace and quiet for reflection and study.

It was during this time that my faithful friend and companion came to me out of the realm of the elemental beings. I was just in the middle of pouring arnica into my foot bath when something or somebody took hold of my hands. Against my will I poured in more than the doctor had prescribed. Within me, I heard the words 'That's how you need your bath.' On the edge of the bowl I noticed a delicate being like a gnome. He was very different from the ones I had met before: fresh and strong, yet tender like the sprouting of leaves in spring, permeated by the radiating power of the sun, or so I experienced him. He was not hardened like the root-man and not airy like the fairies. He had a harmonious effect on me. His feet were as light as wings yet they were the kind that can walk on the earth or, better still, can glide over it without losing touch with the ground, but at the same time were not tied to it.

This gnome was different from all the rest and yet I had come across something like him before. A memory dawned on me. He had helped me to overcome a difficulty in a dream at night. Even more impressively than the roughest root-man, he had shouted at an adversary who was standing in my way. He seemed to be aware of my recollection.

'I will stay with you,' he said. 'You really can't live alone.'

What he said sounded down-to-earth, like a factual statement. And he did indeed stay with me. Over many years, we have grown closer, grown into a sort of lifelong companionship. It is as if we are married.

He is close to me and yet always a bit mysterious. We are no strangers to one another and yet do not know everything about each other. Each lets the other retain their essence and their individuality while remaining united like a single entity.

I do not know his name. It is one of the unspoken secrets. 'Karlik!' I shouted, laughing, when I saw him on the edge of the bowl. That is the Russian word for 'gnome'.

This name pleased him, so that is what he now calls himself in the human world. I realised that for human beings it is exactly the same. When we are born, someone gives us a name. That is what we are called as long as we live. But nobody knows what our eternal being in the other world would be called. Nobody knows their own real name.

Karlik and I are not always together, but we always have each other in mind. Because of this, we can find each other; whether in thought, in picture, or by interpenetrating one another. Otherwise, we each attend to our own work and do our duty as well as we can. Karlik senses whenever I am looking for him. I do not have the wide awake, sometimes super-wakeful consciousness of gnomes. Sometimes I allow myself to be distracted by outer life and do not notice when he wants something. But he can make his presence felt. He takes my hands and guides them so that I misplace just what I need. After my frantic searching he delights in my realising what is the matter and my pleading, 'Karlik, forgive me! I am here for you.'

I then immediately find what was lost. My hands are guided so skilfully, that the time lost in searching is quickly made up again and we are able to carry on a conversation while we are working. No one hears this though, because I speak to gnomes more inwardly in thoughts and feelings, just as I do with plants.

Now and then Karlik says 'Sit down, let's have fun.' Elemental beings regard enjoying themselves as an important activity. Together, we abandon ourselves to feelings of thankfulness for everything in the world that has already become true, beautiful and good. From these feelings of thankfulness we gain strength for new deeds and confidence that what is as yet not good, true and beautiful can become so. Thus we can always improve on what we each have to do, not only in our own occupation but also in our working together with others.

On Karlik's instructions, I soon advised people who did not already know him, to sit down quietly and enjoy themselves. Their reply was often, 'I've no time for anything like that.'

Unfortunately, what Karlik said about that was inaudible to them: 'People have time to be annoyed or pour scorn on somebody or something, therefore they must have time to have fun.'

Karlik and his friends are happy in their work. They dance and laugh through it. One might think they were playing a game, just as I thought I was when I wanted to float away with the elves. But in all their merriment lies seriousness and purpose. Karlik and his friends play a part in what happens on the earth and he told me repeatedly, 'If you understand that and co-operate with us, then many things on earth can be restored to health. Our earth is obviously getting old, but she could last a little while longer if you treated her sensibly.'

Unfortunately, we human beings are not 'sensible', and, as Karlik thinks, 'often not even well behaved.' Our behaviour is painful for the gnomes. We want to possess more and more. Profits and returns are more important to us than the laws of nature. We think too much about ourselves and forget our brothers and sisters in the other realms of nature, even in those that anyone can be aware of, that are visible to us. Karlik and his friends suffer not merely because of human foolishness: there is also what he calls 'the great invisible war', the battle against those elemental beings who no longer want to co-operate and who can no longer take pleasure in what is already true, beautiful and good. They have turned their backs on the earth and mankind. 'They were given nothing,' explained Karlik. 'It feels to them like starving feels to you: they received neither warm human thoughts, nor prayers out in nature, nor even love or thankfulness. People only take and do not give anything, do not give us what we need. Many of us are angry with them.'

Time after time when I tell people about elemental beings, I am reminded of how selfish our behaviour really is. I am often asked, 'How can one influence these beings so that my garden is more productive, or so that agricultural yields will improve? Can your gnome suggest a herb which will make me well again? Can't they do our work for us like in old fairy tales?' Our encounters with such beings are expected to bring advantages. Only rarely does someone ask what we can do for elemental beings, or asks what they feel about our one-sided technical advances. Once someone wants to take part completely selflessly in the life of elemental beings, then Karlik shines and beams with happiness.

I get a lot of pleasure when he beams like this, but also I soon sensed his burning pains within me, shortly after we got to know each other. In a group of people who were studying anthroposophy very seriously, we spoke about the evolution of the earth and of humanity. It was during the time that East and West were beginning the nuclear weapons race. The woman leading the group said apparently without concern, 'If the earth is destroyed, we can still save our eternal self.' I wanted to respond to this, but was so taken aback that I could not find the words. Shortly afterwards, another member of the group expressed the thought that we should be pleased that in East and West there were nuclear weapons, because this would hold the balance between the superpowers. This time I joined in: hesitantly and somewhat inarticulately I expressed the view that this balance is not the only important thing, and that we should consider how our technology affects the realms of nature and the elemental beings. This group had discussed such beings, so I must be able to mention them. The answer was, 'One ought not to be so mystical.'

I wanted to say something in reply, but then I noticed Karlik. He was suffering indescribably. Gnomes cannot cry. But he appeared to be getting ever smaller and more delicate. With the hurt he was suffering he seemed to melt like a lump of sugar in hot tea. I promised we would stay away from such conversations and I told him I would rather belong with him and his friends and not save my 'eternal self'.

For a long time, Karlik remained weak and changed in some way. Had he been a human being, I would have said he was ill. We suffered together and through bearing the suffering together, our friendship deepened and has become a lifelong companionship. Thus real love can unite different beings.

Festivals

What we human beings suffer from has to do with ourselves, with our own incapability, or with our 'becoming', as Karlik would say. One cannot be human without at the same time becoming guilty. Being human means having to learn, and learners make mistakes.

Our mistakes cause pain. Before Karlik came to me, a blue-winged man told me all about this. He is a gnome but he is also like a butterfly. He sets the insects humming with his music. He is their music teacher. With a voice which reminded me of the rustling of the wind in the grass, he whispered to me what he knew of mankind's guilt and suffering.

It became clear to me that we suffer on our own account as human beings, but all of creation that is visible and invisible suffers innocently with us, for us, and because of us. This realisation made me feel depressed. I was ashamed for us all and asked forgiveness. Other realms of the spirit world opened themselves to me. I experienced how what will happen here on earth is prepared in those realms and how what has already happened here goes on working there afterwards. Around every light there were menacing shadows and intense struggles. Someone once said to me that if I could really experience the spirit world, then I must already be in a paradisal situation, free of troubles. That is impossible, because all that becomes visible here is formed there. The spiritual world is not a haven, a little holiday home, in which a person or group of people can stay to get away from everyday troubles.

What ought I to do, and how could I keep going? I often asked myself such questions and it did not occur to me to discuss them with Karlik. His unasked-for answer came spontaneously, 'You should be glad and celebrate festivals. Then you'll find the way.'

This answer to serious life questions is somewhat unexpected for a human being.

'Of course, no one can live in paradise any longer,' added Karlik, 'but festivals are memories, are glimmerings of paradise. They make new life possible. They enable what is becoming. You can only accept the darkness and bear it when again and again you look towards the light. Don't forget that. In the light lie the powers for transformation.'

Human festivals are often empty and tiresome. Many people worry about them beforehand or are disappointed when the special day has gone and yet nothing has happened. The festivals of gnomes are wellsprings of strength, expressions of joy and thanksgiving.

'Festivals are seeds,' said Karlik, 'something new grows from festivals, something good and bright that bears within it the seeds for the next festival.'

Like plants, Karlik's language is alive. He is a leader of the spirits of the medicinal plants and is woven through and through with processes of healing and becoming. He especially loves the festivals of the plants. One of the first in the year is the Festival of Earth Stirrings. This is a celebration of everything in the earth which is creating, moving, rousing itself and becoming. The Earth Stirrings Festival cannot be experienced directly by most people. Nevertheless, they have some inkling of it. The gnomes get busy tending and caring for all that is coming into being. Celebrating festivals and working belong together. Gnomes love their task and experience these celebrations as high points in their creative activity.

With the awakening of spring come various festivals of buds and blossoms. Each kind of plant has its own minder. They organise what we might call family or group festivals. But the joy from such events spreads itself over all the elemental beings who work together for the good of the earth, because they are united in their task. In late summer and autumn there are fruit and seed festivals. The consecration of the seed spirits reminds me of children's christenings.

In the Festival of Ripening there is great dignity, as in encounters with wise, elderly people. Karlik loves the Festivals of the Vegetables. We often experience these together. To him, as a spirit of medicinal plants, the welfare of mankind is a matter of great concern. He loves to help me with cooking, especially when we are expecting guests. Then he guides my hands, just as he did when I was preparing my foot bath. But now I notice it consciously and therefore can be better guided. He sits there cheerfully on the pan handle and advises me. Before preparing the vegetables I arrange them carefully on the table, as if for a harvest thanksgiving. We admire the different shapes. Karlik dances round them all and strokes them with his sunny hands in blessing and offers the vegetables to mankind as nourishment. Only then do I begin the preparation. This kitchen work has something radiant about it. If housewives despise their work, they hurt Karlik.

After the Earth Stirrings Festival, the next big general festival is the celebration of spring at Eastertime, involving lots of dancing. The elves' circle dances are especially beautiful. With dance and music, they mould and tend the flower forms. Their circle dances are serious play for them, a fulfilment of their task. They celebrate the arrival of the spring full moon and the wonderful sunrises. The elemental beings' nature-music sets the birds singing their dawn and evening choruses. 'Human beings can hear that too!' said Karlik joyfully.

In summer comes the great Festival of St John's Tide. The sound of dancing and singing bursts forth in far-reaching waves. The elemental beings fly into the radiant splendour. Now the St John's Tide gnomes fill themselves with golden sunshine. In the autumn they want to give this to the earth. One might call their activity 'harvesting light'. The sun-soaked gnomes of St John's Tide seem round and golden.

Quite soon after St John's comes the Festival of Mist Wisps. These are the admonisher beings. They remind the revellers, 'Come back and start to calm down.' Yet this festival, of wilting and dying, is celebrated joyfully too. People's autumnal sadness seems strange to gnomes. They accept what is and do not resist it. Everywhere a call resounds which could be translated roughly in our words as, 'The visible becomes invisible so that the visible can come into being,' or perhaps as, 'The light fades because it wants to increase.' Elemental beings experience becoming in passing away, and passing away in becoming. They see and affirm life as it really is. It is particularly true of their leaders, those portrayed in fairy tales as elf and gnome kings.

They are the wakeful ones who take the sleepier of their kind into their contemplations.

The November festival could also be called the Festival of Quietness or the Festival of Reflection. Whoever takes part in it learns to rest inwardly. On a certain day, everything goes quiet and only one word is heard: 'Now!' That means: now everyone is back home in the earth. The earth and all within her are satisfied. Now it is the Festival of Inner Peace.

The cycle of the year can be experienced as the earth's breathing. The November festival and the Earth Stirrings Festival are polarities like inhaling and exhaling. St John's Tide represents the culmination of exhalation. After the November festival comes the culmination of inhaling, which is celebrated in the great Festival of the Inner Sun. Preparations for the festival would be made by silent inner rejoicing interspersed with happy shouts of jubilation: 'Soon the sun will shine within the earth, very soon it will be light!' And then all seems to shine and become transparent. Light streams into the earth like liquid gold. All elemental beings who still wish to work for the wellbeing of the earth allow themselves to be penetrated and inspired by this light. At this time they love it when people sing their Christmas carols about the true sun and the inner light.

Then Karlik often says, 'Sit quietly, let's enjoy ourselves.'

After the Festival of the Sun Within the Earth, the moon-lady, a great fairy, begins her dance. She dances in advance what will be danced by the fairies and elves in spring and thus points to the forms of the new plants. She has already danced at the consecration of the seed spirits to show what they should take with them into their dreams. Now she dances and sings in order to awaken the sleepers. She also wakes the gnomes and elves from their devotion to the sun within the earth. Whoever sees the moon-lady and heeds her call, gets the urge to start work on the Earth Stirrings Festival. Out of restfulness come stirrings of activity.

Such festivals shine upon and guide all earth's creation.

'If only people could just tune in so that their deeds are in unison with our work,' says Karlik. 'But their deeds still do not harmonise with what is happening in other realms. There is still a discord in it.'

He is very serious when he speaks like this. 'Of course, the earth is able to last a little longer if you treat her sensibly. She can last until you transform the discord. You have a beautiful place here to learn this.'

I grow sad when I realise how serious he is and how time marches on. But then he caresses me with his sunny hands and with his head. That is what gnomes do if they want to show their love. And he says,

'Look at the light. Again and again look towards the light. That's the only way we can transform the shadows.'

And then the two of us look towards the light and work on, celebrating in cheerful earnest. And the earth is like one great altar.

Mutual Friends
and Acquaintances

As Karlik and I now belong together, we introduce one another to our friends and acquaintances. He is right beside me if someone visits me whom he considers one of his friends or if I am trying to help someone who is in need. He is always present when I run into difficulties during a conversation. He can be with me and yet carry on his work at the same time because he is not limited by space and time.

Karlik especially likes children and is happy when we can tell them stories. Sometimes I allow a 'Karlik gnome' to appear in a story. This always amuses him. He likes it when children play with gnomes and take them with them into their fantasy world. Like this he learns more about the world of children. But he does not always get on so well with adults. He loves all people who also can love, people who can devote themselves to something enthusiastically. He has great affection for all those in real suffering.

45

These he carefully differentiates from people who fuss about each little ache or who indulge themselves in their misery, nursing it to the point of not even wanting to be rid of it. He wants to help the genuine sufferers. He is pleased when many of them bring their problems to us. Listening to them and going into their problems is one of our tasks together.

He has no time for mere theoreticians. He is a clear yet practical thinker. When over-intellectual people come, he withdraws. Sometimes he thumbs his nose as he leaves and I notice this, but fortunately the visitors do not. In doing so he wants to say to me, 'Don't be impressed. He thinks he is always right. But no person is right all the time, least of all him.' Once he withdrew and when he came back he told me about his talk with his friend the 'great gnome' who, like Karlik, is a leader of the elemental beings and one of Karlik's friends. The 'great gnome' he said, laughing mischievously, had told him the following: 'Each person who gives a lecture eventually gets tired and has to stop. It is just as well that everyone gets tired.' The 'great gnome' probably came to this conclusion because many people who gave lectures lived in his surroundings. Karlik likes to repeat the words of the 'great gnome' in front of 'clever' people and he fools around in such a funny way that it is hard for me not to laugh.

On one occasion when I too, with a great deal of effort, wanted to become 'clever', Karlik was furious with me. I will never forget it. I was trying to understand a psychology book and said, 'Karlik, this author would classify you as an archetype.'

Karlik must have sensed my thoughts in all their cold, dead form and detected something like an unconscious doubt about him and his realm. He threatened to leave me if ever I said anything like that again. His rage shook me. This he noticed and his head stroked me. 'You experience me as an image, but I am a being,' he said, 'and you must not think that book seriously but only grasp what's in it.'

'Thinking seriously' for him means to take thoughts as reality without examining them to see if they are correct. With Karlik's intelligence, following the train of thought of a theory without looking for its faults would be immediately obvious to him. I vowed that I would no longer 'think seriously' such books and said that I too often experience people like an image that I make of them for myself, and only very rarely can I penetrate to their real being. After that, things were fine again between us.

Yet I have to mention that Karlik is interested in books. At first he called them 'thought boxes'. He reads them indirectly through me in that he receives the thoughts which I form while reading.

Of course, superficial books are out of the question for him. Much of what is now written is a foreign language to him and when I have to tackle such books he can only shake his head and withdraw.

＿

It is wonderful for me to get to know other elemental beings through Karlik – his friends, that is. He likes most of all to introduce me to those beings which we humans call 'gnomes'. However, in their realm there are so many different kinds. It teems with them. There are the actual gnomes, those especially wise nature spirits who give their name to their entire race. They are dignified earthbound teachers, not continually up to tricks like goblins which we humans classify as gnomes, just as we do all nature beings who are at home in the earthly element.

The dwarves, who are not quite so earthbound, are the various little people who occupy themselves with stones, plants or metals, without being limited to a particular kind. They can be wise like gnomes, but dangerously over-clever too and are often inclined to play all sorts of practical jokes like goblins. Obviously, on account of the fact that they especially like making friends with humans, they also tend to be the most anthropomorphised in pictorial representations. It is about these dwarves that fairy storytellers like to speak most of all. We recognise dwarves from their pointed hats that represent their aura. They point upwards as a force, which can pull away from the earth a little. This is rarely the case with pure gnomes.

Anyone who thinks they can lump all dwarves together is deceiving themselves. There are various dwarf-folk, like wood dwarves, meadow dwarves, little mountain-men, house dwarves such as brownies and so on. And then there are particular types of dwarf in each landscape. Little root-men are nature spirits connected with roots and differ from true gnomes. (There are large and small ones according to the plant species.) Then there are the little earth-men whom we could also call little soil workmen. As close friends of earthworms they work skilfully in the ground, loosening and firming as needed. Leaders of the gnomes work with earth wisdom, little soil workmen with the earth forces.

There are many more kinds still. I only know a small fraction of the vast throng. The term 'man' or 'little man' raises the issue of whether such beings are divided into sexes. Of course they are not. If we anthropomorphise them in pictorial representations, the more powerful beings seem to us more masculine and the gentler ones more feminine. Thus we express a polarity which also determines life in their world.

Thus the root gnome works with the hard, knotty part of the plant, whereas the elves unfold the delicate blossoms.

And the variety of elves is absolutely amazing! Each plant species has its particular elves. And many different elves work on an individual plant, such as colour elves, form elves, scent elves, and eventually during blossoming and fading, the petal elves. There are even sound elves who help a soft nature-music hum in the harmony of the plant. Over all these elves rules the leading spirit of the plant, its architect. Above these plant spirits are the group leaders, amongst whom is Karlik, a leader of the spirits of the medicinal plants. And above these are still higher beings up to the angels of the various seasons.

Likewise, there are so many water nymphs or undines that it is hard to give a general overview. I know little about them, because Karlik does not often have anything to do with them. However, it is easy to imagine a whole variety of water-beings at work: in rain, in a stream, in the sap of a plant, in the sea or in a lake.

Between the distinct kinds of elemental beings are borderline groups which cannot be assigned to a particular element. Earlier we have referred to the water-splasher, who belongs to both the goblins and to the water beings; the blue-winged man, who is like the gnomes and the butterflies; and the winged dwarves of St John's Tide. It is not possible to say whether moss-wights or bud dwarves belong more to gnomes or to elves.

I cannot present a report on elemental beings like a researcher in natural science or even science of the spirit. I know their world only so far as my experience reveals it to me. In this respect I regard it my duty to thank them in loving devotion for all they have given us, deputising for people who know nothing about them, or who have never even considered that these beings need our love and attention. By telling stories and modelling, I try as best I can to build a bridge from the human world to that of elemental beings. Again and again, some people have had the goodwill to cross this bridge and approach the nature spirits in their thoughts and feelings. My invisible friends notice this and it pleases them.

Reminiscences

It is not possible for me to put all my experiences with elemental beings in writing. However, I would like to say a little more about a few of them that are clear in my mind.

For a long while I had the job of planning programmes for the blind on Basel Radio. During the first recording, I was nervous in the soundproofed studio, and felt abandoned by the whole world. Of course, I couldn't, like sighted people, see the other staff nearby through the glass panels. Yet I was not alone. By the way, we are never alone; we are always surrounded by invisible beings. There was a gnome-like being in the microphone who gawped at me cheekily. When I spoke it grinned at me mockingly and flustered me. Gnomes are wise, but the gnome-like beings in machines are too clever by half. They are cleverer than the most crafty of the dwarves. So clever are they, that their cleverness holds them fast in a pitiable condition.

'Don't let him put you off, just speak in his direction.' I recognised these thoughts as good advice from Karlik, whom I had not had in mind while I was tense and nervous. After the session, the producer wanted to know how I was able to speak into the microphone despite his having forgotten to show me where it was. I was taken aback by this, because I was used to hiding my inner experiences from others. 'It was... it was...' I stammered and then breathed a sigh of relief as he answered his question himself, 'It was a coincidence.'

Karlik laughed. Then the thought occurred to me: strange, here's someone who ascribes coincidence to the spiritual world, which gives us everything. I am always sorry for the gnome-like beings in machines. Somehow they too seem to belong to the elemental beings but they are cut off from all that is living, as if trapped in the machine as an idea that has become concrete, in the realisation of which they have worked with all their over-cleverness. They are prisoners of themselves and they get even less attention than other elemental beings from the people they serve. I really must take the trouble to keep them in mind and thank them for their work. This does not come to me as spontaneously as it does with the other elemental beings.

The schoolroom where I had to teach was dismal and the working atmosphere was frosty. It was a school for adults and they worked without enjoyment or interest.

I was chilled to the marrow and lost all courage. There was a building site not far away. Often we had a job to make ourselves heard over the noise of the pneumatic drill. But Karlik could speak as he normally did. 'Come to the window and look,' came his voice within me. I obeyed. 'Look there, right below the window.'

And indeed, just below us were scented flowers and elves hovering in a dance, busy at their work. 'Can you really lose courage when they are still dancing here and letting the flowers bloom in this place?' asked Karlik.

No, I could not. I resolved to persevere and work with all the elemental beings who are forever doing the best they can in our urban environments. Strengthened and inspired by their example, I resumed my work. When approached in the right way, contact with elemental beings brings an ability to cope with life and not a dreaminess or remoteness from the world. Now I had learnt from the elves how enjoyable it is to work even under difficult circumstances, and I no longer tried to fly away from my body to avoid life's problems. Properly cultivating our contact with elemental beings means learning something new from them, and thus becoming increasingly fitter for the fulfilment of our common task.

Once I was in a forest and a branch brushed my face and hair. 'The tree greets you with his feet,' laughed Karlik.

I did not understand what he was trying to tell me. Then he explained it to me: to gnomes, people are upside-down plants and plants are upside-down people. People's feet are on the ground. That does not apply to plants. Their roots are their heads. Therefore their heads are in the ground. And they grow towards the sky from their heads. What we call the 'crown' of a tree is its foot. Little root-men are wise. They surround the root-heads of the plants with thoughts. Elves are beings of movement. They surround the feet of the plants with dances.

I pondered this: viewed this way human beings must grow in reverse, from heaven to earth. Indeed, small children have large heads which are already well developed and which could be envisaged as roots. One could say that they grow into their feet. But, with this picture in mind: are humans really supposed to grow from heaven to earth?

Karlik answered the question I was pondering: 'Mankind is supposed to bring the heavenly world to earth. Thus they must grow into their feet.' I thought of a child who brought heaven to earth in a way that no ordinary child could ever do, and I told Karlik about it. He always likes to hear this story at Christmas.

Later, I found in Rudolf Steiner's writings references to human beings as inverted plants. It was confirmation of the reality of my own experiences. Karlik was very satisfied with the 'thought box' which contained what he already knew in another way.

As we got to know each other, I soon wanted to find out from Karlik why the earth has become so hard and fixed. Why could it not be shining, permeated and driven by life, just like the world that I experienced when I left my body in full consciousness. Karlik often replies to questions which I or others would like to have answered by saying, 'You will get to know why only when you are supposed to. So learn to wait. Then it will come to you.'

When I asked again, 'Couldn't the earth be any different?' there came the abrupt answer, 'No, it couldn't.'

Once my mother asked me to help her with the jam-making. I stood by the stove and stirred. Karlik took his place on the pan handle. As the jam cooled and became thicker he began to dance and shout: 'It was like that! It was like that!'

I asked, 'What was?'

'Like that, with the earth,' he shouted, and it came to him like a joyful memory. 'It was just like that and now you know.'

I was pleased with his joy but I could not understand what he wanted to tell me until some time afterwards. In anthroposophical books, set out in clear scientific thoughts, I discovered what Karlik had wanted to show me allegorically about the development of the earth.

How beautifully thoughts and allegories complement each other and together, lead to a real living knowledge. The occasion for discovering this was a practical task in the kitchen. Now I realise, we are all here to learn.

What Karlik says and what I experience with him, takes shape within me as the imagery of fairy tales. Consequently, Karlik contributes to the form of my wax models and to my stories. But he also likes stories which are told especially for him, ones that are meant as a gift to him. I do not tell them audibly, only in thoughts and feelings, in the same way as I speak to the flowers I am watering.

I tell him one of his favourite stories as follows: 'Our earth is a great seed placed amongst the great multitude of stars. Innumerable stars flourish, some fade and others flourish anew. But we cannot tell what the earth-seed should become. This is hidden within it like a secret. Sometimes it seems as if nothing can come of it, but in a seed what will eventually appear of course remains invisible. The secret of the earth-seed is love. Often it seems as if there is none. Indeed, something quite the opposite seems to hide in this seed. But again and again some light glimmers through the earth-seed and gives us the hope through which we can persevere. Again and again when good appears in the natural world and among mankind, little lights gleam brightly on earth. These are the first small deeds of love that we sometimes succeed in doing. And one day the earth-seed will shine out with the Festival of the Inner Sun. You know that better than I do. When we take good care of this great seed amongst the stars, when we carefully unfold its secret and allow more and more love to shine out as little points of light on the earth, then it will one day flourish as the most beautiful of all the stars.'

Just like children, gnomes want stories repeated exactly without alteration. They love repetitions. If Karlik is present during the housework I hum melodies which humans would find monotonous. But gnomes love note sequences which are constantly repeated. They hear music in cow bells or in the rustling of the wind in the trees.

Through our activities and conversations together I learnt to pay attention to the quality of time, to the rhythm of the constantly recurring cycle of days and seasons. Karlik is not aware of clock or calendar time, of any time which can be externally quantified. For him, the coming and going of a day is like the blossoming and fading of a flower. Together with him I let the awakening morning affect me gently and, from the increasing light, take my cue to grow into the duties of the day. Or, I let the parting day draw to a close within me and, thankfully, go round my apartment once again to say goodnight to the flowers and objects.

It reminds me of childhood holidays in the Alps. Before going to sleep it was the custom to chant the alpine prayer and all would feel safe and sound. I learnt from Karlik that it is not only possible but also very necessary to say this evening prayer in an urban dwelling.

Through our shared life, new things constantly arise within me. Our path together through the cycle of days and seasons gives me strength and confidence. Giving and receiving flows vigorously between us. That is how we are, even if we are often separated in our work, we are still constantly and firmly connected.

Lord of the Elements
Interweaving Christianity and Nature

Bastiaan Baan

In this unique book, Bastiaan Baan brings the four classical elements together with ideas from Rudolf Steiner's anthroposophy. He considers, in particular, how elemental beings relate to these, and explores the role of elemental beings in our world.

This is a fascinating and original work by an experienced spiritual thinker on the connections between Christianity and the natural world.

florisbooks.co.uk

The Spirit of Trees
Science, Symbiosis
and Inspiration

Fred Hageneder

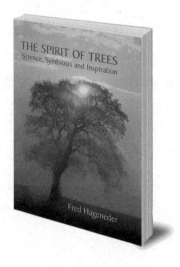

Trees are one of Earth's oldest life forms, yet many people today are unaware of their significance.

This book captures all these elements in an inspiring holistic appraisal, beautifully illustrated in colour. Hageneder looks in detail at twenty-four of Europe and North America's best-loved trees: their physical characteristics, their healing powers, the traditions associated with them and how they have inspired human beings through the ages.

florisbooks.co.uk

 Floris
Books

For news on all our **latest books,**
and to receive **exclusive discounts,**
join our mailing list at:

florisbooks.co.uk

Plus subscribers get a FREE book
with every online order!